On the Decay of the
Art of Lying

Billy Liar
Erith Playhouse
10th-15th October 2016

WHAT I

bemoan IS

THE GROWING

prevalence

OF THE

BRUTAL *truth.*

Mark Twain

ON THE DECAY
OF THE ART OF
Lying

AMERICAN ROOTS

Applewood Books
CARLISLE, MASSACHUSETTS

The short works Applewood includes in its American Roots series have been selected to connect us. The books are tactile mementos of American passions by some of America's most famous writers. Each of these has meant something very personal to me.

When I was growing up my grandfather advised me: "Dress British, but think Yiddish." It was good counsel and this has ruled me most of my life. The advice, of course, suggested that I learn to build an exterior that belied my interior. I can only imagine what Mark Twain would have thought about this, but for me it was a call to practice a high art of lying. We live in an age where Truth and Trust are sisters. But while everyone is clamoring for transparency, sometimes a filter of color softens the light and brings comfort and warmth to those friends, family, acquaintances, and passersby who need it most.

"What I bemoan is the growing prevalence of the brutal truth."

&Phil Zuckerman
PUBLISHER

Observe, I do not mean to suggest that the *custom* of lying has suffered any decay or interruption,—no, for the Lie, as a Virtue, a Principle, is eternal; the Lie, as a recreation, a solace, a refuge in time of need, the fourth Grace, the tenth Muse, man's best and surest friend, is immortal, and cannot perish from the earth while this Club remains. My complaint simply concerns the decay of the *art* of lying. No high-minded man, no man of right feeling, can contemplate the lumbering and slovenly lying of the present day without grieving to see a noble art so prostituted. In this veteran presence I naturally enter upon this theme with diffidence; it is like an old maid trying to teach nursery matters to the mothers in Israel. It would not become me to criticize you, gentlemen, who are nearly all my elders—and my superiors, in this thing—and so, if I should here and there *seem* to do it, I trust it will in most cases be more in a spirit of admiration than of fault-finding;

indeed if this finest of the fine arts had everywhere received the attention, encouragement, and conscientious practice and development which this Club has devoted to it, I should not need to utter this lament, or shed a single tear. I do not say this to flatter: I say it in a spirit of just and appreciative recognition. ⟦It had been my intention, at this point, to mention names and give illustrative specimens, but indications observable about me admonished me to beware of particulars and confine myself to generalities.⟧

No fact is more firmly established than that lying is a necessity of our circumstances,—the deduction that it is then a Virtue goes without saying. No virtue can reach its highest usefulness without careful and diligent cultivation,—therefore, it goes without saying, that this one ought to be taught in the public schools—at the fireside—even in the newspapers. What chance has the ignorant, uncultivated liar against the educated expert? What chance have I against Mr. Per—against a lawyer? *Judicious* lying is what the world needs. I sometimes think it were even better and safer not to lie at all than to lie injudiciously. An awkward, unscientific lie is often as ineffectual as the truth.

Now let us see what the philosophers say. Note that venerable proverb: Children and fools *always* speak the truth. The deduction is plain—adults and wise persons *never* speak it. Parkman, the historian, says, "The principle of truth may itself be carried into an absurdity." In another place in the same chapter he says, "The saying is old that truth should not be spoken at all times; and those whom a sick conscience worries into habitual violation of the maxim are imbeciles and nuisances." It is strong language, but true. None of us could *live* with an habitual truth-teller; but thank goodness none of us has to. An habitual truth-teller is simply an impossible creature; he does not exist; he never has existed. Of course there are people who *think* they never lie, but it is not so,—and this ignorance is one of the very things that shame our so-called civilization. Everybody lies—every day; every hour;

awake; asleep; in his dreams; in his joy; in his mourning; if he keeps his tongue still, his hands, his feet, his eyes, his attitude, will convey deception—and purposely. Even in sermons—but that is a platitude.

In a far country where I once lived the ladies used to go around paying calls, under the humane and kindly pretence of wanting to see each other; and when they returned home, they would cry out with a glad voice, saying, "We made sixteen calls and found fourteen of them out,"— not meaning that they found out anything against the fourteen,—no, that was only a colloquial phrase to signify that they were not at home,—and their manner of saying it expressed their lively satisfaction in that fact. Now their pretence of wanting to see the fourteen—and the other two whom they had been less lucky with—was that commonest and mildest form of lying which is sufficiently described as a deflection from the truth. Is it justifiable? Most certainly. It is beautiful, it is noble; for its object is, *not* to reap profit, but to convey a pleasure to the sixteen. The iron-souled truth-monger would plainly manifest, or even utter the fact that he didn't want to see those people,—and he would be an ass, and inflict a totally unnecessary pain. And next, those ladies in that far country— but never mind, they had a thousand pleasant ways of lying, that grew out of gentle impulses, and were a credit to their intelligence and an honor to their hearts. Let the particulars go.

The men in that far country were liars, every one. Their mere howdy-do was a lie, because *they* didn't care how you did, except

they were undertakers. To the
ordinary inquirer you lied in
return; for you made no conscientious diagnostic of your case,
but answered at random, and
usually missed it considerably. You
lied to the undertaker, and said
your health was failing—a wholly
commendable lie, since it cost
you nothing and pleased the
other man. If a stranger called and
interrupted you, you said with
your hearty tongue, "I'm glad
to see you," and said with your
heartier soul, "I wish you were
with the cannibals and it was
dinner-time." When he went,

you said regretfully, "*Must* you go?" and followed it with a "Call again;" but you did no harm, for you did not deceive anybody nor inflict any hurt, whereas the truth would have made you both unhappy.

I think that all this courteous lying is a sweet and loving art, and should be cultivated. The highest perfection of politeness is only a beautiful edifice, built, from the base to the dome, of graceful and gilded forms of charitable and unselfish lying.

What I bemoan is the growing prevalence of the brutal truth. Let us do what we can to eradicate it. An injurious truth has no merit over an injurious lie. Neither should ever be uttered. The man who speaks an injurious truth lest his soul be not saved if he do otherwise, should reflect that that sort of a soul is not strictly worth saving. The man who tells a lie to help a poor devil out of trouble, is one of whom the angels doubt-less say, "Lo, here is an heroic soul who casts his own welfare in jeopardy to succor his neighbor's; let us exalt this magnanimous liar."

An injurious lie is an uncommendable thing; and so, also, and in the same degree, is an injurious truth—a fact that is recognized by the law of libel.

Among other common lies, we have the *silent* lie—the deception which one conveys by simply keeping still and concealing the truth. Many obstinate truth-mongers indulge in this dissipation, imagining that if they *speak* no lie, they lie not at all. In that far country where I once lived, there was a lovely spirit, a lady whose impulses were always high and pure, and whose character answered to them. One day I was there at dinner, and remarked, in a general way, that we are all liars. She was amazed, and said, "Not *all*?" It was before "Pinafore's" time so I did not make the response which would naturally follow in our day, but frankly said, "Yes, *all*—we are all liars. There are no exceptions." She looked almost offended, "Why, do you include *me*?" "Certainly," I said. "I think you even rank as an expert." She said "Sh'sh! the children!" So the subject was changed in deference to the children's presence, and we went on talking about other things. But as soon as the young people were out of the way, the lady came warmly back to the matter and said, "I have made a rule of my life to never tell a lie; and I have never departed from it in a single instance." I said, "I don't mean the least harm or disrespect, but really you have been lying like smoke ever since I've been sitting here. It has caused me a good deal of pain, because I'm not used to it." She required of me an instance—just a single instance. So I said—

"Well, here is the unfilled duplicate of the blank, which the

Oakland hospital people sent to you by the hand of the sick-nurse when she came here to nurse your little nephew through his dangerous illness. This blank asks all manners of questions as to the conduct of that sick-nurse: 'Did she ever sleep on her watch? Did she ever forget to give the medicine?' and so forth and so on. You are warned to be very careful and explicit in your answers, for the welfare of the service requires that the nurses be promptly fined or otherwise punished for derelictions. You told me you were perfectly delighted with this nurse—that she had a thousand perfections and only one fault: you found you never could depend on her wrapping Johnny up half sufficiently while he waited in a chilly chair for her to rearrange the warm bed. You filled up the duplicate of this paper, and sent it back to the hospital by the hand of the nurse. How did you answer this question—'Was the nurse at any time guilty of a negligence which was likely to result in the patient's taking cold?' Come—everything is decided by a bet here in California: ten dollars to ten cents you lied when you answered that question." She said, "I didn't; *I left it blank!*" "Just so—you have told a *silent* lie; you have left it to be inferred that you had no fault to find in that matter." She said, "Oh, was that a lie? And *how* could I mention her one single fault, and she is so good?—It would have been cruel." I said, "One ought always to lie, when one can do good by it; your impulse was right, but your judgment was crude; this comes of unintelligent practice. Now observe the results of this inexpert deflection of yours. You know Mr. Jones's Willie is lying very low with scarlet-fever; well, your recommendation was so enthusiastic that that girl is there nursing him, and the worn-out family have all been trustingly sound asleep for the last fourteen hours, leaving their darling with full confidence in those fatal hands, because you, like young George Washington, have a reputation—However, if you are not going to have anything to do, I will come around to-morrow and we'll attend the funeral together, for, of course, you'll naturally feel a peculiar interest in Willie's case—as personal a one, in fact, as the undertaker."

But that was not all lost. Before I was half-way through she was in a carriage and making thirty miles an hour toward the Jones mansion to save what was left of Willie and tell all she knew about the deadly nurse. All of which was unnecessary, as Willie wasn't sick; I had been lying myself. But that same day, all the same, she sent a line to the hospital which filled up the neglected blank, and stated the *facts*, too, in the squarest possible manner.

Now, you see, this lady's fault was *not* in lying, but in lying injudiciously. She should have told the truth, *there*, and made it up to the nurse with a fraudulent compliment further along in the paper. She could have said, "In one respect this sick-nurse is perfection—when she is on the watch, she never snores." Almost any little pleasant lie would have taken the sting out of that troublesome but necessary expression of the truth.

Lying is universal—we *all* do it. Therefore, the wise thing is for us diligently to train ourselves to lie thoughtfully, judiciously; to lie with a good object, and not an evil one; to lie for others' advantage, and not our own; to lie healingly, charitably, humanely, not cruelly, hurtfully, maliciously; to lie gracefully and graciously, not awkwardly and clumsily; to lie firmly, frankly, squarely, with head erect, not haltingly, tortuously, with pusillanimous mien, as being ashamed of our high calling. Then shall we be rid of the rank and pestilent truth that is rotting the land; then shall we be great and good and beautiful, and worthy dwellers in a world where even benign Nature habitually lies, except when she promises execrable weather. Then—But am I but a new and feeble student in this gracious art; I cannot instruct *this* club.

Joking aside, I think there is much need of wise examination into what sorts of lies are best and wholesomest to be indulged, seeing we *must* all lie and we *do* all lie, and what sorts it may be best to avoid—and this is a thing which I feel I can confidently put into the hands of this experienced Club—a ripe body, who may be termed, in this regard, and without undue flattery, Old Masters.